VENICE

A PICTURE BOOK TO REMEMBER HER BY

Designed and Produced by
TED SMART and DAVID GIBBON

CRESCENT BOOKS
NEW YORK

INTRODUCTION

Many cities, the world over, have inspired the artist's brush, musician's baton and writer's pen, but none quite so passionately as Venice. For fifteen centuries it has graced the shallow lagoon in the North-West Adriatic, gradually emerging as a pinnacle of splendour, and echoes of Shakespeare, Canaletto and Vivaldi fill the streets and waterways of this astonishing city.

Built on a cluster of more than a hundred small islands; towers, domes and palaces rise suddenly from the water, from whichever angle it is approached. Away from the palaces, the "back streets" are an intricate network of narrow canals lined with houses with doors opening onto the water. Venice seems to float in a pool of timeless serenity, defying the 20th century to smother the atmosphere created by its watery environment and splendid architecture that spans hundreds of years.

Inevitably, some concessions have been made, mainly for economic reasons. The Grand Canal is reminiscent of any main road, as a confusion of boats weave expertly in and out of the side canals, their owners shouting directions, and as the vaporetto, Venice's main form of public transport, chugs domineeringly along, passing under the white grandeur of the Rialto Bridge, to and from St Mark's Square. Gondolas, the city's most obvious link with the past, used to be the Venetians' only form of transport, but now they are for the tourist who will want to, at least once, become part of a scene that has been portrayed in books and films everywhere.

In its time, Venice has fallen under the possessive rule of many countries. It was during the 5th and 6th centuries that people fled Italy's shores when Barbarians invaded after the downfall of the Roman Empire, and huts were erected on the mud banks that still support Venice today. Originally under the influence of the East, the election of the first Doge in 697 was approved by Byzantium, as were the first laws. Subsequently under French and Austrian rule, it was finally reunited with the Italian kingdom, but not before enormous wealth had passed through its hands. Wealth that is invested in its magnificent buildings.

Much of this history can be traced in the Piazza San Marco, at one time the world's most famous square. Renaissance columns, arcades and friezes line three of its sides, while the fourth, refuting all academic good taste, hosts the great Basilica of St Mark, the massive bell-tower or Campanile and the intricate, mosque-like Doge's Palace.

That the Palace itself could involve a lifetime's study is a growing awareness in the minds of all visitors, as they wander through the numerous squares, past any one of the 107 churches, or across one of the many bridges. The Venetians love detail. They also love showing Venice off. If a random walk is attempted with the intention of arriving at San Marco, even the most ardent map reader will undoubtedly lose his way, although the city's perimeter is only eight and a half miles and no matter how many times the corner is turned and the bell-tower is spotted in one particular direction. Certainly a delightful way to get to know Venice, but eventually help must be sought, and most Venetians, proud of their city, will set off, seemingly the wrong way, to arrive, only minutes later, in the square.

Sadly though, Venice is not immortal. In sharp contrast to its beauty, crumbling foundations, peeling plaster and towers leaning at odd angles are openly visible, a stark reminder that the floods that have always threatened the streets and squares are causing irreparable damage. Venice is sinking. But not without a fight, as the concern of its millions of enchanted visitors may well ensure that this treasured city remains.

Dedicated to the Evangelist St Mark, the magnificent Basilica *left* dominates one side of the Piazza San Marco. Dominating the nearby Wharf *overleaf,* one of two granite columns is surmounted by a bronze statue of the Winged Lion, the official symbol of the Venetian Republic.

The wide basin of San Marco, where the most important waterways of communication flowed together, was the site chosen as the political, social and religious heart of Venice, and since the 9th century, the Palace of the Doge has lined the waterfront *above*, also claiming the corner of St Mark's Square known as the Piazzetta, where sits the massive Bell Tower, some 300ft high. At the mouth of the Grand Canal, one of the most characteristic main streets in the world, stands the white-domed Church of Santa Maria della Salute *above right*, overlooking the Dogana da Mar (Customs House) built at the point where the Grand Canal and Guidecca Canal divide. Further along, the Grand Canal is lined with colourful houses *far right* and crossed by numerous back canals that weave their way around the whole city, connected by stone and wrought-iron bridges *right* and made accessible by small motor boats and the traditional gondola *overleaf*.

he beautiful square of St Mark contains
variety of architecture reflecting the
fluences of the city's dramatic change
om Eastern to Western leadership. The
d-brick Bell Tower *left* is an exact replica
the original which collapsed in 1902, a
rprisingly harmonious neighbour of the
asilica *below*. Thronged by tourists,
nny cafés provide the perfect meeting
ace *above and right* while *overleaf* is
ptured a rare moment when the square
deserted, except by a cleaner and a
attering of pigeons.

By day, sunlight plays on the intricate
structure of the Basilica *above left,* and
musicians provide traditional open-air
entertainment *below,* while by night the
whole square is bathed in a pool of golden
light *above and right.* The commercial
centre of Venice is the Rialto with its
famous bridge arching over the Grand
Canal *left,* displaying the shuttered backs
of stalls in the busy street market inside.
Amid the red-tiled roofs *overleaf* can be
seen 'altana' where washing is hung out to
dry.

Venice is a cluster of more than one hundred tiny islands that are united by an ingenious network of canals and bridges *these pages*. As a form of public transport, gondolas have been supplanted by steam and motor boats and now their popularity lies almost solely with the tourist. A view down the Rio de Greci *left*, reveals the sloping tower of the Renaissance Church of San Giorgio, and *overleaf* is pictured the Santa Maria della Salute, both built by Longhena.

Colourful houses open onto one of the many small squares *above left* that nestle behind the Grand Canal *above, below and right,* which is characterised by its more glamorous buildings, striped mooring pole and famous landmarks such as the Rialto Bridge *left and overleaf,* where buildings were first erected to house traders' merchandise.

The Clock Tower in St Mark's Square
below is a Renaissance building of the
15th and 16th centuries, built in two
stages from the centre outwards. The
timepiece is marked with the signs of the
zodiac and the upper terrace is noted for
its two Moors *left* – bronze, mechanical
figures that strike the bell to mark the
hours – overlooked *right* by one of the
stately bronze horses on the Basilica's
West façade. The square itself *above*
displays its distinctive markings on marble
slabs, while *overleaf* the state-built votive
Church of Santa Maria della Salute sits
behind the golden-globed Customs House,
dominating the entrance to the Grand
Canal.

Illustrating the richness and power that once belonged to Venice is the Clock Tower's magnificent zodiac timepiece *below*; the Doge's Palace *right* in the Piazzetta, which contains a splendid courtyard *above* and clock *below left*, and the Stairway of the Giants *above left* facing the main entrance of the Porta della Carta. Typical of a wealth of fine mosaics that dress the walls of the Basilica, is the 'Universal Judgement' *overleaf* above the principal portal.

Scenes reminiscent of Canaletto paintings: of drifting romantically past colourful houses, under charming little bridges and relaxing in the sunshine *these pages and overleaf,* act as reminders that Venice is not only a living museum, but a city of vitality that is full of exciting entertainment.

The contrasting images portrayed on *these pages and overleaf* capture a Venice that is universally recognised, even to the uninitiated. The Basilica was completed in 1073 as a replacement for the original church of the Doge's Palace. The four magnificent bronze horses above the main entrance are of Greek origin, and all five portals are surmounted by five arches faced with mosaics that glow against a golden background. Embellishment over the years with the loot of conquests, resulted in the interior and exterior being garnished with golden turrets, ivory and marble. Against a traditional taste, the massive Campanile *right* blends in such a way that only the Venetians know how. Away from the palatial splendour, sunlight dances on the water of quaint canals lined with houses that, despite their obvious dilapidation, display a unique charm. The decorative bridges, arching perfectly between the houses and the narrow streets, perform a vital function in linking together the latticework canals.

The gondolier, with his characteristic water-craft *these pages*, is a figure famed the world over and represents Venice at its most romantic. Over the centuries the size of the gondola has varied greatly, but its classic shape has always been retained and consists of some 280 pieces of wood.

The steps outside the Doge's Palace *overleaf* lead to the Ponte della Paglia (Bridge of Straw) across the Rio di Palazzo.

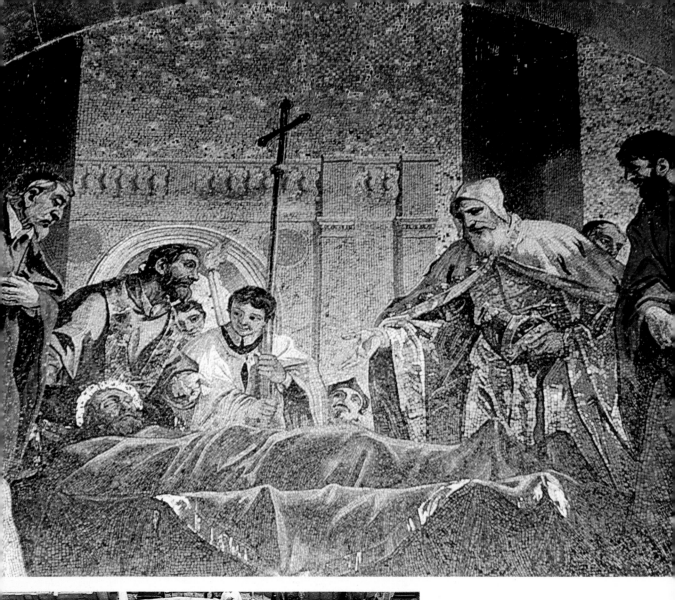

The interior of St Mark's Basilica is shaped in the form of a Greek cross, and ninety-three feet above the floor, five mosaic-lined cupolas glow in a soft, golden light. The 12th-century design of the Dome of the Pentecost *right* represents the Divine Spirit descending upon the Apostles in the form of rivers of fire. In one of the portal lunettes *above*, is depicted Venetians paying homage to the body of St Mark. The grand Central Doorway *left* is composed of three great arches graced with rows of columns and antelamic carvings.

Overleaf: Along a route lined with spectators and brightly-coloured mooring poles, gondolas take part in one of the many regattas that delight visitors throughout the year. The craft are specially made for racing and are called gondolini, but the shape remains similar to those used for tourists.

As the busy Rialto Market continues its day's trading *below*, crowded vaporettos *right* chug up and down the Grand Canal which is lined with elegant houses and colourful blooms *overleaf.* An exploration of the back canals *left and above right* leads to exciting nooks and crannies but also reveals the crumbling foundations of a sinking city. The Bridge of Sighs *above* joins the Ducal Palace to the New Prisons beyond the Rio.

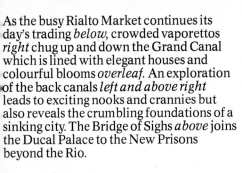

Venice has long been a favourite spot of artists, and the delightful canal scene *below right* and colour-washed Church of San Giorgio *left* are perfect for the sensitive touch of the painter's brush. Resplendent as it guards the basin of San Marco, the gilded sphere *above* surmounts the Dogana da Mar, built by the architect Giovanni Benoni. The monument *below* commemorates the patriot Paolo Sarpi, whilst *above right* a series of arches and small columns decorate the spiral staircase (bovolo) of the Contarini del Bovolo Palace in the Calle della Vida.

The Basilica of St Mark *overleaf,* suffused in a golden light, shimmers under a violet sky.

e churches of San Moisé *left* and San
dal *below* have foundations dating back
ne ten centuries. The Procuratie Vecchie
St Mark's Square *above* was built over a
riod of 60 years and is a fantastic creation
50 arches on the ground floor and twice
t many windows on the upper floors.
ored gondolas *overleaf*, soon to be
en out on the turquoise waters of the
nals *right*, line the San Marco basin
terfront.

The Church of Santa Maria della Salute *left and right*, San Giorgio *below* and the Doge's Palace *above right* are just some of the temptations of Venice. A photographer *above* is anxious to catch the beauty of St Mark's Basilica and all the while shops and cafés line the Grand Canal *overleaf* – all reminders of the splendour of this 'floating' city.

First published in 1981 by Colour Library International Ltd.
Illustrations and text © : Colour Library International Ltd, 163 East 64th Street, New York 10021.
Colour separations by FERCROM, Barcelona, Spain.
Display and text filmsetting by Focus Photoset, London, England.
Printed by Cayfosa and bound by Eurobinder - Barcelona (Spain)
Published by Crescent Books, a division of Crown Publishers Inc.
ISBN 0-517-250233
Library of Congress Catalogue Card No. 81 82935
CRESCENT 1981